# Crafts for Easter

# Crafts for
# EASTER

## by Kathy Ross
### Illustrated by Sharon Lane Holm

Holiday Crafts for Kids
The Millbrook Press
Brookfield, Connecticut

For Greyson and Allison—K.R.
To Michael—S.L.H.

Library of Congress Cataloging-in-Publication Data
Ross, Kathy (Katharine Reynolds), 1948-
Crafts for Easter / by Kathy Ross : illustrated by
Sharon Lane Holm.
p. cm. —(Holiday crafts for kids)
Summary: Presents 20 simple crafts for springtime and Easter
that young children can make from everyday materials.
ISBN 1-56294-918-7 (lib. bdg.) ISBN 1-56294-268-9 (pbk.)
1. Easter decorations—Juvenile literature. 2. Handicraft—
Juvenile literature. [1. Easter decorations. 2. Handicraft.]
I. Holm, Sharon Lane, ill. II. Title. III. Series.
TT900.E2R67   1995
745.594'1—dc20   95-13510   CIP   AC

Published by The Millbrook Press
2 Old New Milford Road
Brookfield, Connecticut  06804

# Contents

# Happy Easter!

Easter always falls on a Sunday in March or April, but it can be on a different date each year. It is celebrated on the first Sunday after the first full moon following the first day of spring, the twenty-first of March.

For Christians, Easter is the joyous time when they remember that Jesus Christ came back to life. Many people who are not Christian also take part in traditional Easter activities. Children expect a visit from the Easter Bunny, who hides decorated eggs for them to find. Children may wake up and discover a basket filled with candy, often brightly colored jelly beans or chocolate eggs.

Easter can be a celebration of springtime, when animals are born and flowers appear again after the cold winter months. Pink tulips and yellow daffodils, baby chicks and lambs, new outfits and bright hats—Easter celebrates new life.

# Stuffed Bunny Friend

Everybody loves the Easter Bunny!
Here is a bunny for you to make.

## Here is what you need:

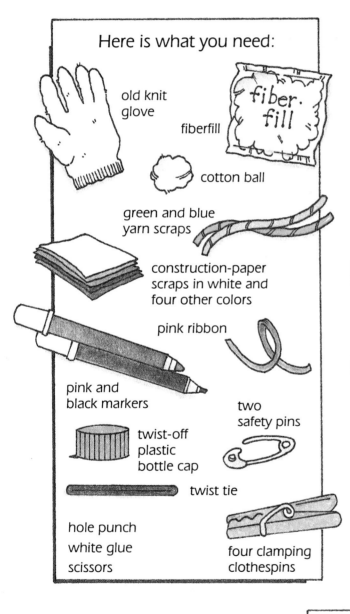

old knit glove

fiberfill

cotton ball

green and blue yarn scraps

construction-paper scraps in white and four other colors

pink ribbon

pink and black markers

twist-off plastic bottle cap

two safety pins

twist tie

hole punch
white glue
scissors

four clamping clothespins

## Here is what you do:

**1.** Fold back the middle finger of the glove and use the safety pin to pin the finger to the hand from the inside of the glove. Stuff the remaining fingers, the thumb, and the hand of the glove with fiberfill.

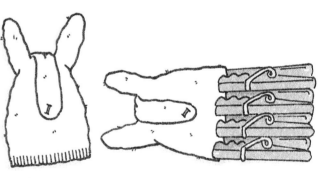

**2.** Fold about 1 inch (2.5 centimeters) of the bottom edge of the glove to the inside. Glue the bottom opening of the glove and hold the bottom together with clothespins until the glue is dry.

**3.** Make a basket for the bunny by covering the sides of the bottle cap with pink ribbon. Fill the cap half full with glue. To form a handle, stick the two ends of the twist tie into the glue on each side of the cap. Fill the cap with snips of green yarn. Squeeze more glue on top of the yarn and glue in some eggs punched from papers of different colors. Let the basket dry.

**4.** Pull the thumb and little finger of the glove forward to form the bunny's arms. Slide the basket over the little finger and safety-pin the thumb and finger together from behind so that the pin doesn't show. Slide the basket over the area where the thumb and little finger join.

**5.** Tie a pink bow just above the folded arms to define the bunny's neck. Cut paper circles for eyes and put dots in the centers with a marker. Glue them on. Make whiskers by forming a knot in the middle of two pieces of blue yarn and unraveling the ends. Glue the whiskers below the eyes. Glue a cotton-ball tail on the back of the bunny at the tip of the folded-down finger. If the glove you used is a light color, color the center of the ears pink with a marker.

You can also hang the basket on a long piece of ribbon to make a very pretty necklace.

# Pull Tab Rabbit Necklace

Make this necklace for yourself or to give as a gift.

## Here is what you need:

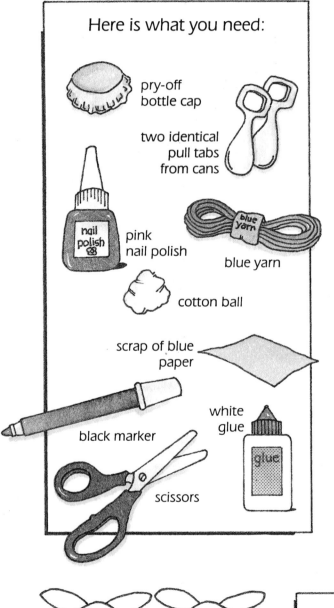

pry-off bottle cap

two identical pull tabs from cans

pink nail polish

blue yarn

cotton ball

scrap of blue paper

black marker

white glue

scissors

## Here is what you do:

**1.** Paint the pull tabs and the outside of the bottle cap with the nail polish and let them dry.

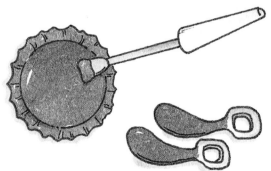

**2.** Fill the cap with glue and place the rings of the two pull tabs inside the cap so that the tabs stick out like rabbit ears.

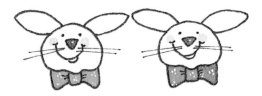

Cut a piece of yarn 2 feet (.6 meter) long and put both ends in the glue between the rings. Cut a thin circle from the cotton ball and gently press it over the rings and the glue in the cap.

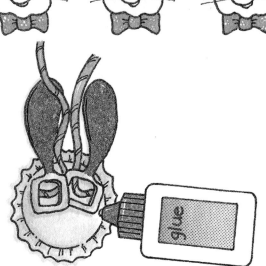

**3.** Cut two tiny eyes from blue paper and make dots in the middle of each one with a marker. Glue the eyes on the cotton ball below the ears. Knot a short piece of blue yarn in the middle and fray both ends to make whiskers. Glue the whiskers below the eyes.

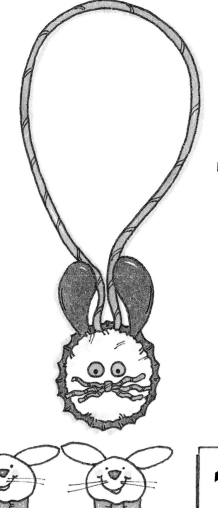

This bunny also makes a very nice refrigerator magnet. Instead of adding the yarn hanger, just press a piece of sticky magnetic strip on the back of the bunny.

# Necktie Bunny Puppet

Old neckties make great puppets.

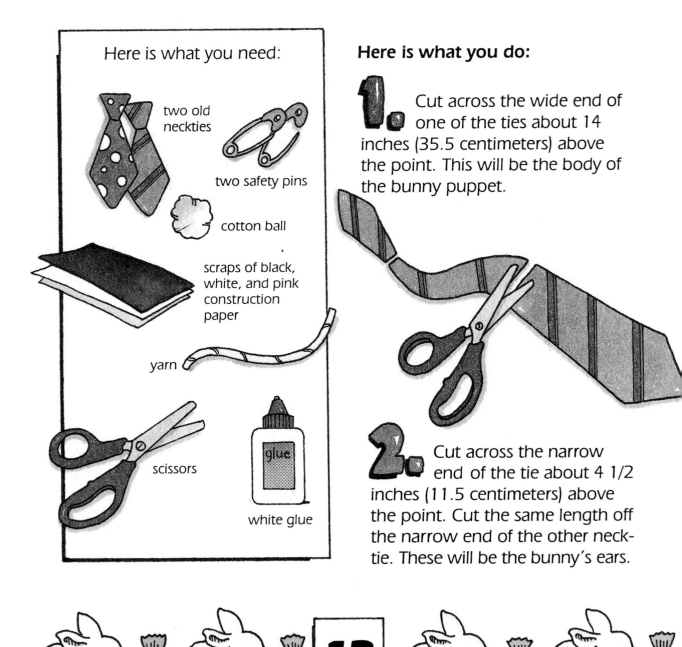

## Here is what you need:

two old neckties

two safety pins

cotton ball

scraps of black, white, and pink construction paper

yarn

scissors

white glue

glue

## Here is what you do:

**1.** Cut across the wide end of one of the ties about 14 inches (35.5 centimeters) above the point. This will be the body of the bunny puppet.

**2.** Cut across the narrow end of the tie about 4 1/2 inches (11.5 centimeters) above the point. Cut the same length off the narrow end of the other necktie. These will be the bunny's ears.

**3.** Cut a heart-shaped nose from pink paper. To form whiskers, glue two pieces of yarn to the point of the wide part of the tie. Glue the nose over the middle of the whiskers. Cut two eyes from the black and white paper and glue them above the nose.

**4.** About 2 inches (5 centimeters) above each eye, cut a small slit. The slits should be just long enough so that the straight ends of the ears, if slightly bunched up, will fit into them. Pin the ears to the body with safety pins, hiding the pins in the folds of the ears.

**5.** Glue a cotton-ball tail to the body of the bunny and let the glue dry.

To work the puppet, slip your hand between the fabric and lining of the necktie all the way to the point. Fold the head down. The bunny's ears will stand up and allow you to make many different expressions. Hold your bunny tight! Don't let him hop away!

# Giant Bunny Basket

This giant bunny basket makes an unusual Easter decoration. Fill the basket with your favorite stuffed bunnies, chicks, ducks, and some big plastic eggs to make an eye-catching display.

## Here is what you need:

carton of the size and shape you want your basket to be

pink, blue, and white construction paper

fiber fill

fiberfill

rubberband

two brown 12-inch (30-centimeter) pipe cleaners

12-inch (30-centimeter) paper plate

two 6-inch (15-centimeter) paper bowls

paintbrush

white glue

glue

masking tape

scissors

newspaper to work on

cellophane tape

## Here is what you do:

**1.** To make the bunny's cheeks, glue the rims of two bowls to the back of the paper plate. Cut bunny ears from the white and pink paper. Glue the ears to the top of the plate.

**2.** Use the paintbrush to cover the plate and the bowls with glue. Then cover the plate and bowls completely with fiberfill.

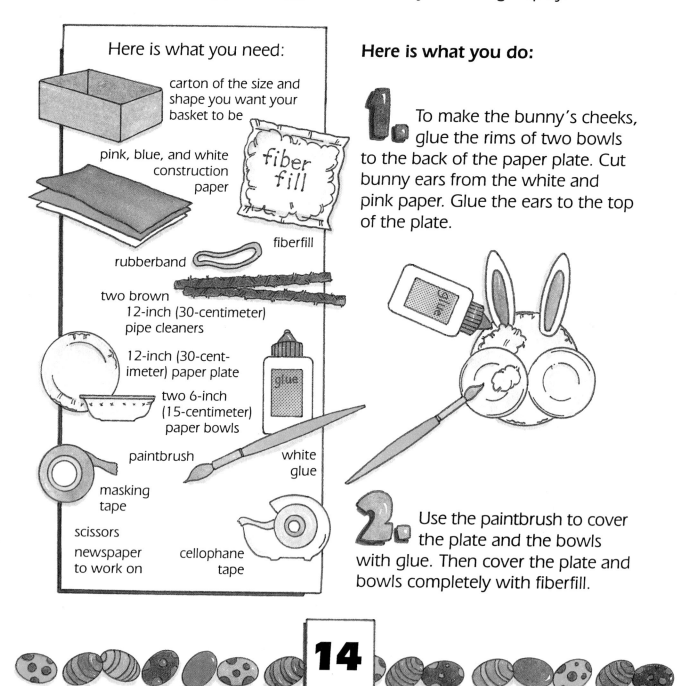

**3.** Twist two pipe cleaners together to form whiskers. At their centers, glue them to the middle of the plate. Also use a piece of masking tape to hold the whiskers in place. Cut a nose out of the pink paper and glue it over the tape. Cut eyes out of the blue and white paper and glue them above the nose. Let the bunny head dry completely before continuing.

**4.** Fold the flaps to the inside of the carton. Glue the head to one end of the carton. Use your paintbrush to cover the outside of the rest of the carton with glue. (Don't glue the bottom.) Cover the glued outside with fiberfill.

**5.** To make the bunny's tail, bunch some fiberfill into a ball and then wrap it with a rubberband to keep its shape. Glue the tail to the back of the bunny.

**6.** Cut a handle from construction paper and glue the two ends inside the basket. Hold the ends in place with cellophane tape while the glue dries.

If you like, now you can fill the basket with Easter grass.

# Wallpaper Easter Basket

This pretty little basket is so easy to make you could give one to each of your friends.

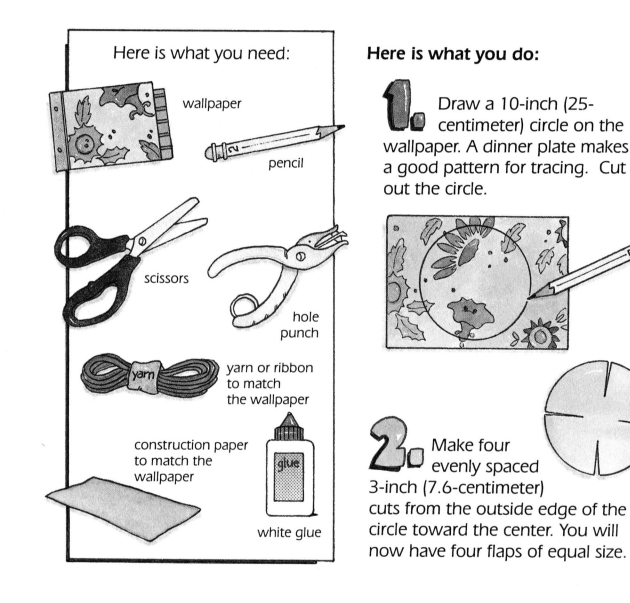

## Here is what you need:

wallpaper

pencil

scissors

hole punch

yarn or ribbon to match the wallpaper

construction paper to match the wallpaper

white glue

## Here is what you do:

**1.** Draw a 10-inch (25-centimeter) circle on the wallpaper. A dinner plate makes a good pattern for tracing. Cut out the circle.

**2.** Make four evenly spaced 3-inch (7.6-centimeter) cuts from the outside edge of the circle toward the center. You will now have four flaps of equal size.

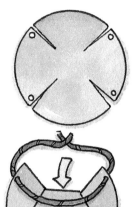

**3.** Punch two holes, about 1/2 inch (1.25 centimeters) from the edges of two flaps that are across from each other.

**4.** Cut two pieces of yarn 6 inches (15 centimeters) long. String one piece of yarn through the two holes directly across from each other on opposite flaps. Pull the two flaps together, with the yarn around the outside of the flap between them. Tie the yarn in a bow. Punch two holes and string the other strand of yarn through the flaps on the other side in the same way and pull the circle up into a basket.

**5.** Cut a long rectangle from construction paper to make a handle and glue the two ends inside the basket.

Fill the basket with Easter grass and some special Easter goodies.

# Easter Basket Party Hat

This is an Easter basket to wear on your head!

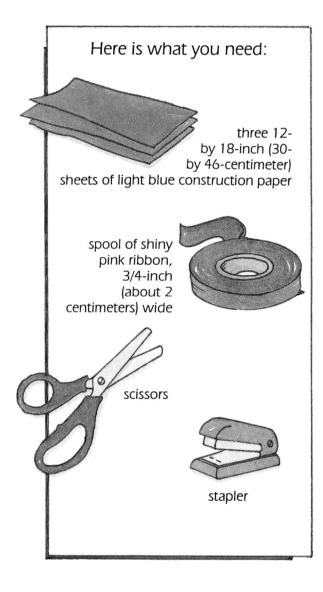

## Here is what you need:

three 12-
by 18-inch (30-
by 46-centimeter)
sheets of light blue construction paper

spool of shiny
pink ribbon,
3/4-inch
(about 2
centimeters) wide

scissors

stapler

## Here is what you do:

**1.** Fold two sheets of the construction paper in half lengthwise. Staple the ends of the two sheets together to make a band of paper long enough to fit snugly around your head. Be sure the ends overlap slightly and trim off any extra paper.

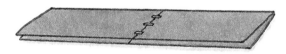

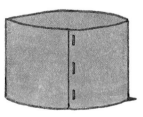

**2.** Now fold the band of paper in half lengthwise again and cut 4-inch-long (10-centimeter-long) slits about 1 inch

(2.5 centimeters) apart all the way along the band. Do not cut through the folded edge of the paper.

Unfold the band and weave three rows of ribbon through the band to make it look like a basket. Staple the ends of the ribbon to hold them in place. Fold the top of the basket over the ribbon about 1 1/2 inches (4 centimeters) and staple it in place to give the basket a neat top edge. Staple the ends of the woven band together to complete the hat.

Cut a strip of blue construction paper to make a handle. Cover it with a strip of pink ribbon and staple the ribbon in place. Make a bow from the ribbon and staple it to the handle.

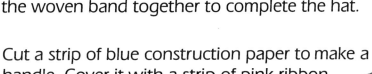

Staple the ends of the handle to the inside of the basket hat.

Don't let a mixed-up bunny put any eggs in this basket!

# Basket Full of Easter Friends

Did something in your Easter basket wiggle?

## Here is what you need:

old knit glove

orange, yellow, white, and pink felt scraps

fine-point marker

yarn in three different colors

cotton balls

white glue

scissors

stapler

yellow paint

paintbrush

two 6-inch (15-centimeter) paper plates

newspaper to work on

## Here is what you do:

**1.** Cut out half of the center of each plate. This makes a basket shape. The uncut half forms the basket, and the cut half forms the handle. Place the two plates together, bottoms facing outward, and staple the sides to form a basket. Leave the bottom open. Paint both sides of the basket yellow and let it dry.

**2.** Stuff a cotton ball into each finger of the glove. Tie a piece of yarn in a bow under each cotton ball to hold it in place. This makes a little head at the end of each finger.

**3.** Turn the fingers into rabbits, chicks, and ducks by cutting eyes, ears, and beaks from bits of felt and gluing them on the heads. Use yarn knotted in the middle and frayed on the ends to make whiskers for the rabbits. Let the glue dry before trying out the puppets.

Put your hand in the glove. Slide the glove into the basket so that the Easter friends are peeking over the basket rim. Can you think of a name for each of your five new animal friends?

# Basket Egg Holder

Make a holder to display your prettiest decorated egg.

## Here is what you need:

plastic cover from spray can with an inner plastic ring

12-inch (30-centimeter) pink pipe cleaner

masking tape

yellow yarn

thin pink and yellow ribbon or yarn

Easter sticker or small picture cut from a greeting card

Easter egg

white glue
scissors

small paintbrush

Easter grass

## Here is what you do:

**1.** Wrap the outside of the plastic cover with masking tape. Spread glue over the masking tape with the paintbrush. Starting at the bottom of the cover, carefully wrap yellow yarn around the entire outside. Glue an Easter sticker or a small picture cut from a greeting card to the side of the cover. Let the glue dry.

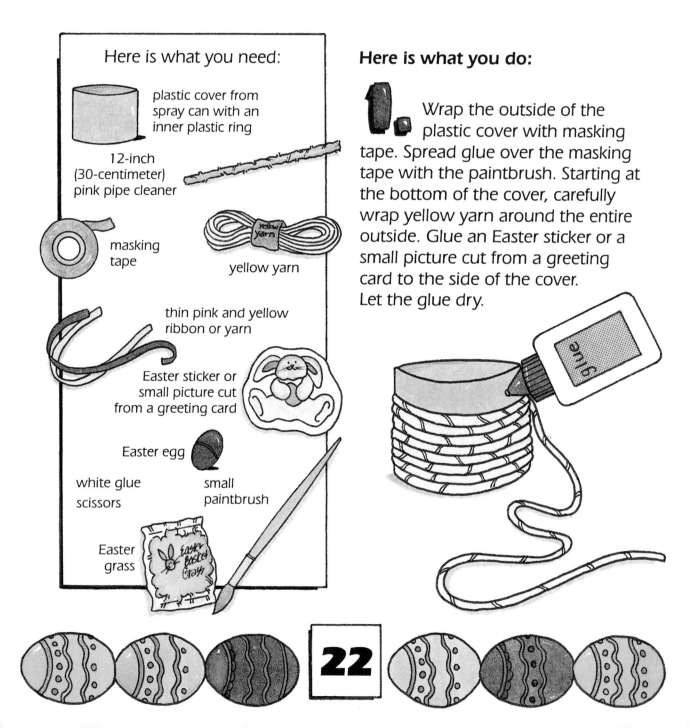

**2.** Tape each end of the pipe cleaner inside the cover to form a handle for the basket. Tie yellow and pink ribbon or yarn into a bow on the handle. Tuck some Easter grass into the basket.

To display one special Easter egg, stand the egg on its end in the inner ring of the plastic cover.

# Easter Egg Memory Game

Here is an Easter game to make and play with a friend.

## Here is what you need:

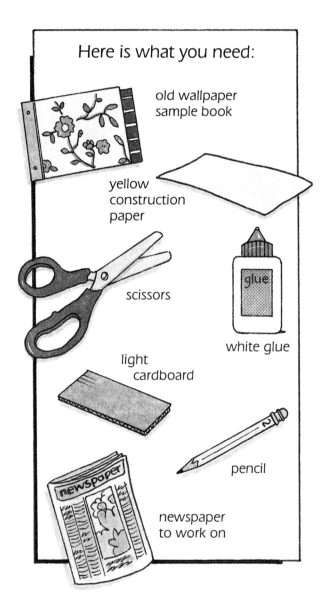

old wallpaper sample book

yellow construction paper

scissors

white glue

light cardboard

pencil

newspaper to work on

## Here is what you do:

**1.** Sketch an egg shape about 3 1/2 inches (9 centimeters) tall onto the cardboard with a pencil. Cut out the egg shape. This is your pattern.

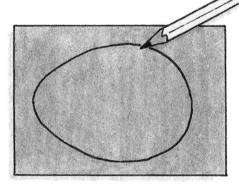

**2.** Use the pattern to trace twenty-two eggs onto the yellow construction paper. Cut out the eggs. Choose eleven different wallpaper designs from the wallpaper book. Using your egg pattern, cut out two eggs from each design.

**3.** Glue a yellow egg to the blank side of each wallpaper egg and let the eggs dry flat. If the edges start to curl, put some heavy books on top to weigh them down while they dry.

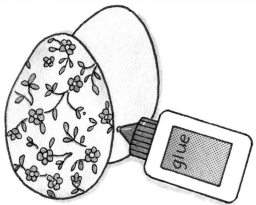

To play your Easter Egg Memory Game, you will need two players. Put all the eggs yellow-side-up on the floor or a table. The first player turns two eggs over. If they match, the player gets to keep them. If they do not match, the player must turn them yellow-side-up again, and it's the other player's turn. To match eggs, each player must remember where the different patterns are hidden. After all the eggs have been turned over, the winner of the game is the player with the most matched sets of eggs.

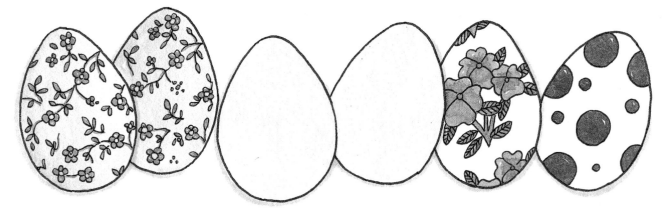

To make this game more difficult, just make more pairs of eggs. The eggs must be yellow on one side, but the other side can be made with wrapping paper, wallpaper, or different colors of construction paper, or can be decorated with crayons or markers. Remember, there must be two eggs of every color or design. Make sure you always play with an odd number of pairs of eggs, too, so that there will always be a winner.

# Easter Egg Matching Card

Make this Easter card to give to a younger brother, sister, or friend.

## Here is what you need:

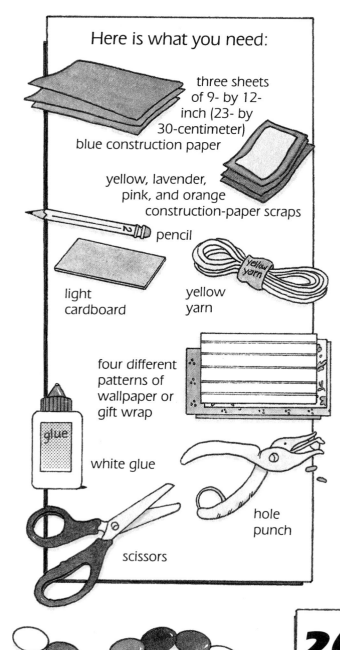

three sheets of 9- by 12-inch (23- by 30-centimeter) blue construction paper

yellow, lavender, pink, and orange construction-paper scraps

pencil

light cardboard

yellow yarn

four different patterns of wallpaper or gift wrap

white glue

hole punch

scissors

## Here is what you do:

**1.** Cut the three sheets of blue construction paper in half to make 9- by 6-inch (23- by 15-centimeter) rectangles. Put two of the sheets aside. Lay the other four sheets on top of each other. Cut the sheets in half to form eight 3- by 9-inch (7.5- by 23-centimeter) strips. Make two stacks of four strips each.

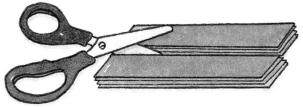

**2.** Place one of the 9- by 6-inch (23- by 15-centimeter) sheets of blue paper behind the strips. The strips will make the top and bottom pages of the card. The uncut sheet is the cover. Punch four holes along the center of the card and lace the yarn through them to tie the cover and strips together. Do not tie the yarn too tightly or it will be hard to turn the pages.

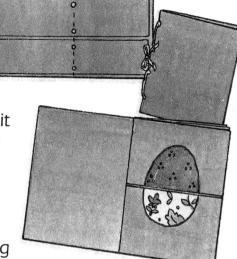

**3.** On cardboard, sketch an egg about 3 1/2 inches (9 centimeters) long. Cut it out to use as a pattern to make eight different eggs from the construction paper and the wallpaper. Cut each egg exactly in half widthwise. Glue the top of an egg on the top strip of the first page. Glue the bottom of a different egg on the bottom strip of the page, carefully lining up the halves to form a complete egg when the two strips are together. Glue a different egg bottom on each bottom strip, lining each one up with the top half of the egg on the first page. Go back to the beginning of the card. Glue the egg tops to the rest of the strips. Be sure each page has an egg with a different top and bottom.

**4.** Decorate the front of the book with more Easter eggs. On the cover, write "Here is an Easter game for you! Help the Easter Bunny match the tops to the bottoms of his Easter eggs."

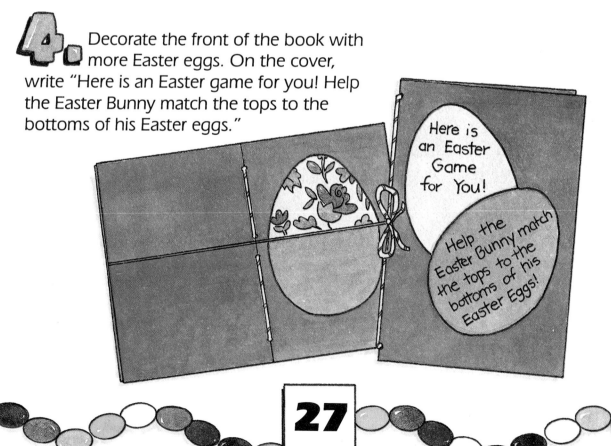

# Giant Foil Egg

Make this giant egg to hang on your front door.

## Here is what you need:

light cardboard

aluminum foil

pipe cleaners

permanent markers

cellophane tape

ribbon

white glue

scissors

## Here is what you do:

1. Cut a large egg out of cardboard. Make it at least 12 inches (30 centimeters) long.

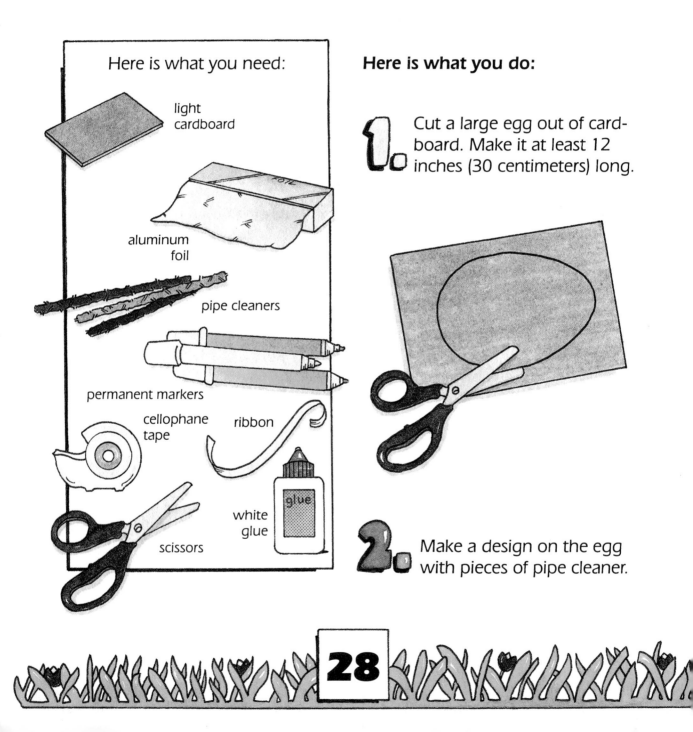

2. Make a design on the egg with pieces of pipe cleaner.

Glue on circles, lines, zigzags, and other shapes. Let the glue dry completely before continuing.

**3.** Carefully cover the egg with foil. Press the foil down over the pipe cleaners on the egg so that the design shows clearly. To hold the foil in place, tape it to the back of the egg.

**4.** Use permanent markers to color in or around the designs on the foil egg to make the designs stand out.

**5.** To make a hanger, tape a piece of ribbon to the top of the egg.

# Three-Envelope Easter Chick

This Easter chick has a surprise inside.

## Here is what you need:

three greeting-card envelopes of the same color and size

yellow, blue, and black construction-paper scraps

scissors

white glue

marker

## Here is what you do:

**1.** Glue two envelopes, turned lengthwise with their flaps open and to the outside, to the back of the third envelope. They may overlap slightly. These flaps will be the chick's wings. Fold the flaps of each envelope over the ends of the third envelope. Trim off the excess that sticks up over the top of the center envelope. These pieces will become baby chicks.

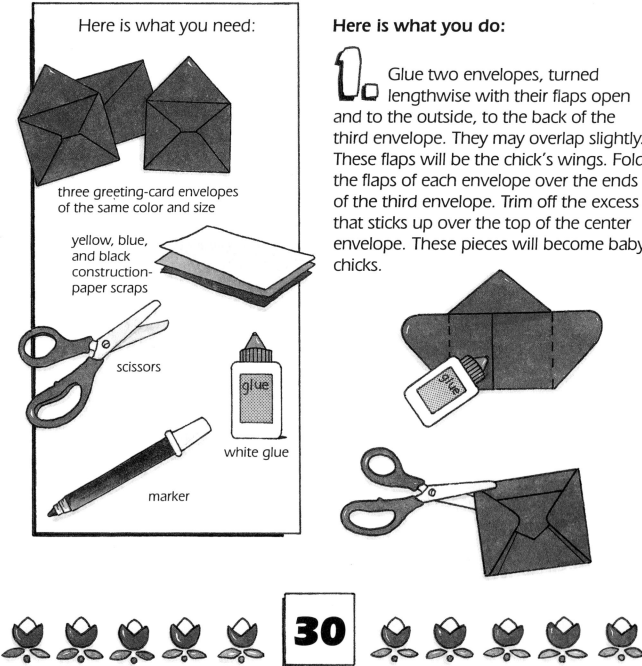

**2.** Unfold the two wings. Cut eyes and a beak from construction-paper scraps and glue them on the flap of the middle envelope to form a face. Glue the eyes so that the wings will cover them when the wings are closed.

**3.** Cut beaks and eyes from paper scraps and glue them on the flaps of the two extra pieces to make faces for the baby chicks. Write an Easter message on the bodies of the chicks and then tuck them into the middle envelope. Fold the head of the large chick over the babies, then fold the wings over the face.

If you used white envelopes for this project, color the chicks with crayons or markers.

# Fluffy Pinecone Chick

Did that pinecone just "peep?"

## Here is what you need:

- large, fat pinecone
- pencil
- yellow paint
- fiberfill
- paintbrush
- white, blue, orange, and yellow felt scraps
- green construction paper
- Easter grass
- white glue
- newspaper to work on
- scissors

## Here is what you do:

**1.** Paint the pinecone yellow and let it dry.

**2.** Wrap the pinecone in a thin layer of fiberfill, using a pencil to poke the fluff between the scales of the pinecone.

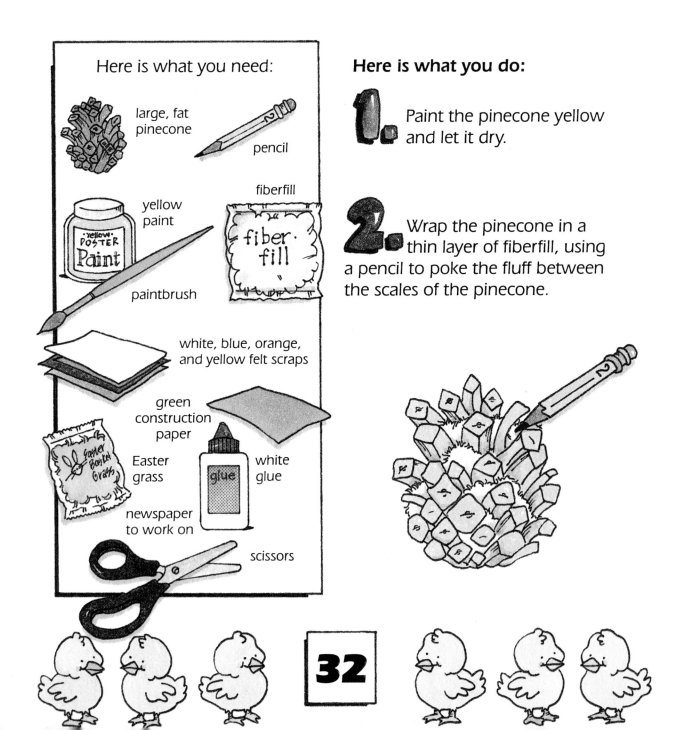

**3.** Cut wings, a beak, and eyes from felt scraps and glue them on the pinecone body.

**4.** Cut a 4-inch (10-centimeter) circle out of green construction paper. Glue Easter grass on top of the circle. Then glue the pinecone chick to the middle of the grass.

This little chick makes a very nice table decoration.

# Hanging Easter Basket Chick

Here's another Easter chick, but this one is really a basket!

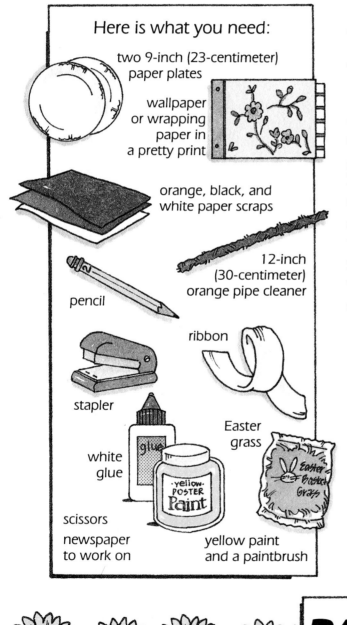

## Here is what you need:

two 9-inch (23-centimeter) paper plates

wallpaper or wrapping paper in a pretty print

orange, black, and white paper scraps

12-inch (30-centimeter) orange pipe cleaner

pencil

ribbon

stapler

white glue

Easter grass

scissors

newspaper to work on

yellow paint and a paintbrush

## Here is what you do:

**1.** Hold two paper plates together, bottoms outward. Fold an orange pipe cleaner in half and insert it partway between the plates so that both halves stick out. Staple the rims of the plates together, three quarters of the way around, leaving the top open. Fold the two ends of the pipe cleaner to shape them into chick feet. Fold the top edges of both plates to the outside and staple them open.

 Paint the plates yellow and let them dry.

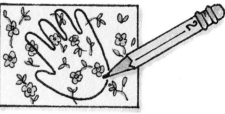

 Trace the shape of your hands onto pretty paper and cut out the paper hands. Glue the hands on each side of one of the plates to form wings. Cut eyes and a beak from paper scraps and glue them in place.

4. Staple the ends of the ribbon between the plates on each side of the opening to make a hanger for the basket. Stuff the chick with Easter grass.

Fill this basket with Easter treats. Hang it on the doorknob of the door of someone special!

# Tennis Ball Chick Puppet

If you drop this little chick, it just might bounce away!

## Here is what you need:

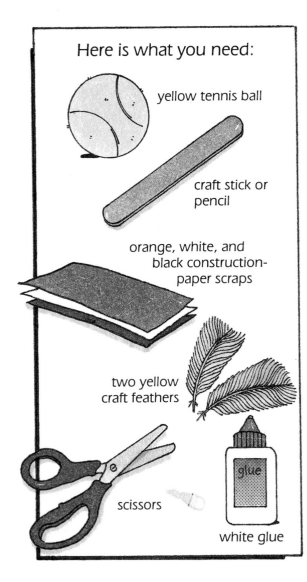

yellow tennis ball

craft stick or pencil

orange, white, and black construction-paper scraps

two yellow craft feathers

scissors

white glue

## Here is what you do:

**1.** Ask a grown-up to cut a 2-inch (5-centimeter) slit in the tennis ball with a sharp knife.

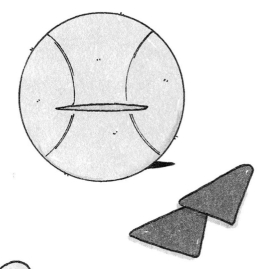

**2.** Cut two triangle-shaped pieces for the chick's beak from orange paper. Rub glue onto the top and bottom edges of the

slit in the ball. Glue the edges of the triangles to the slit to form the top and bottom of the beak. Slide the craft stick or pencil between the top and bottom triangles and leave it there until the glue has dried so that the triangles are not glued shut.

**3.** Cut eyes from black and white paper scraps and glue them in place above the beak. Glue two craft feathers to the back of the chick to make a tail. Let the glue dry before using the puppet.

To make the chick's mouth move, just squeeze the ball on each side of the beak. This chick can be used as a party favor, too. Fill it with tiny toys and wrapped candy.

# Spring Lamb

Make this lamb to decorate your room for spring.

## Here is what you need:

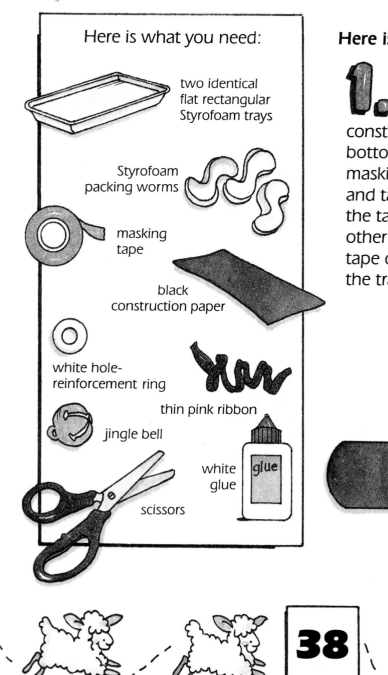

two identical flat rectangular Styrofoam trays

Styrofoam packing worms

masking tape

black construction paper

white hole-reinforcement ring

thin pink ribbon

jingle bell

white glue

glue

scissors

## Here is what you do:

**1.** Cut a head, legs, and a tail for the lamb from black construction paper. Cover the bottom of one Styrofoam tray with masking tape. Glue the head, legs, and tail and ribbon for a hanger to the tape. Cover the bottom of the other tray with tape. Cover the tape on both trays with glue. Glue the trays together.

**2.** Stick the white hole-reinforcement ring on the head for an eye and glue on an ear cut from black paper. String the jingle bell on the pink ribbon and tie it in a bow around the lamb's neck.

**3.** Cover the front tray with masking tape, then cover the tape with glue. Stick Styrofoam packing worms all over the tray to give the lamb a woolly coat.

Hang this lamb up quickly! He might follow you to school one day!

# Handprint Lamb Easter Card

Turn your hand into a lamb to make this special Easter card.

## Here is what you need:

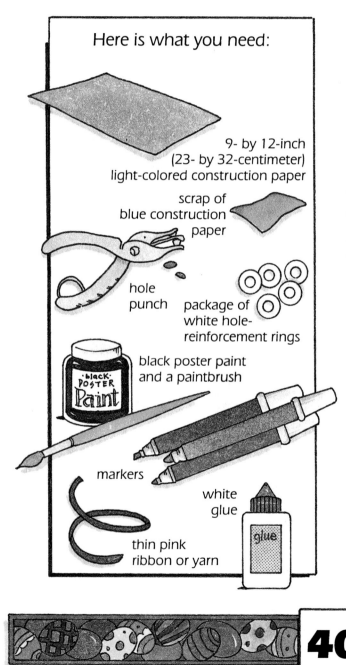

9- by 12-inch (23- by 32-centimeter) light-colored construction paper

scrap of blue construction paper

hole punch

package of white hole-reinforcement rings

black poster paint and a paintbrush

markers

white glue

thin pink ribbon or yarn

## Here is what you do:

**1.** Fold the construction paper in half to form a 6- by 9-inch (15- by 23-centimeter) card. Paint your palm black with the poster paint. Make a handprint on the front of the card with your fingers and thumb spread apart and pointing toward the bottom of the card. Let the handprint dry before you continue.

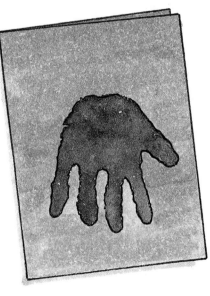

 Cover the hand part of the handprint with the hole-reinforcement rings to make the lamb's woolly coat. The four fingers will be the lamb's legs, and the thumb will be the head.

**3.** Use the hole punch to make an eye for the lamb from blue paper. Make a dot in the middle of the eye with a marker and glue the eye to the thumb of the handprint. Glue a pink ribbon bow to the neck of the lamb.

**4.** Use markers to add grass, flowers, and a sun. Inside the card, write "Happy Easter from your little lamb" and sign your name.

People you love will enjoy receiving cards made from your handprint.

# Easter Bonnet Wall Hanging

This Easter bonnet goes on the wall, not on your head.

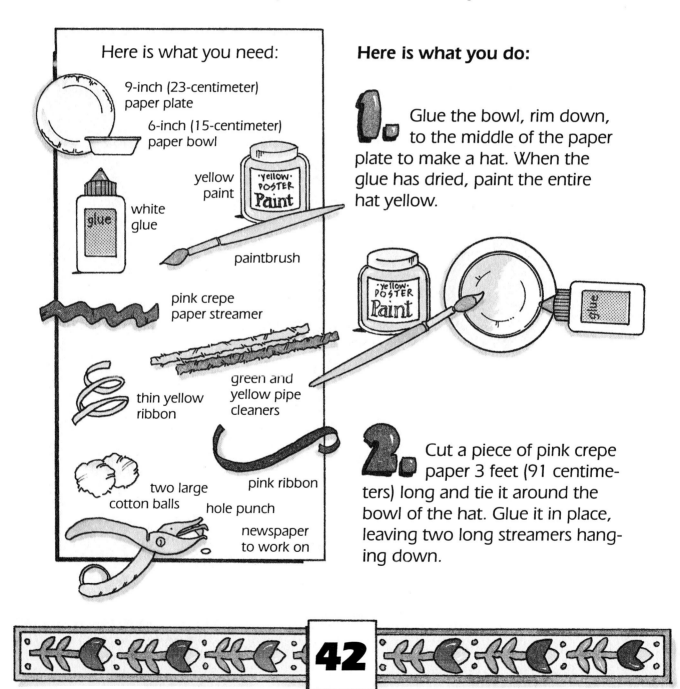

## Here is what you need:

- 9-inch (23-centimeter) paper plate
- 6-inch (15-centimeter) paper bowl
- yellow paint
- white glue
- paintbrush
- pink crepe paper streamer
- green and yellow pipe cleaners
- thin yellow ribbon
- pink ribbon
- two large cotton balls
- hole punch
- newspaper to work on

## Here is what you do:

**1.** Glue the bowl, rim down, to the middle of the paper plate to make a hat. When the glue has dried, paint the entire hat yellow.

**2.** Cut a piece of pink crepe paper 3 feet (91 centimeters) long and tie it around the bowl of the hat. Glue it in place, leaving two long streamers hanging down.

**3.** Make two flowers to decorate the hat. To make each flower, bend a 2-inch (5-centimeter) piece of yellow pipe cleaner in half. Poke the bend in the pipe cleaner through a cotton ball and pull the cotton up around the pipe cleaner to form a flower. Bend the two ends of the folded pipe cleaner to make the stamens at the center of each flower.

**4.** Insert a 6-inch (15-centimeter) piece of green pipe cleaner into the fold of the yellow pipe cleaner to make the stem of the flower. Join the two flowers together by wrapping a 12-inch (30-centimeter) green pipe cleaner around the stems and then folding its ends into the shapes of leaves. Tie a pink bow around the flowers and glue them to the hat just above the streamers.

**5.** Punch a hole in the rim of the hat on the side opposite the streamers. Tie a piece of thin yellow ribbon through the hole to form a hanger.

You can make an Easter corsage with the same kind of flowers you made to decorate this hat.

# Designer Easter Outfit

This project lets you design the Easter outfit of your dreams.

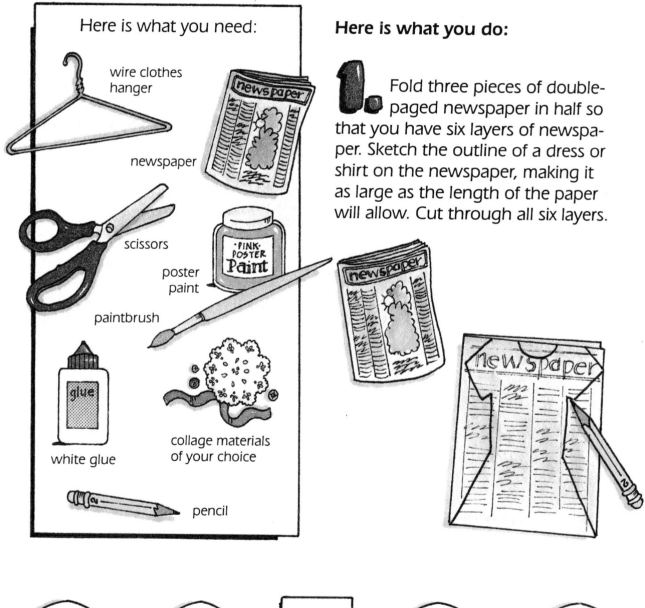

### Here is what you need:

- wire clothes hanger
- newspaper
- scissors
- poster paint
- paintbrush
- white glue
- collage materials of your choice
- pencil

### Here is what you do:

**1.** Fold three pieces of double-paged newspaper in half so that you have six layers of newspaper. Sketch the outline of a dress or shirt on the newspaper, making it as large as the length of the paper will allow. Cut through all six layers.

**2.** Slip a wire hanger between the layers of the outfit at the shoulders so that three layers of newspaper are in front of the hanger and three layers are in back. Squeeze some glue between each layer of newspaper so that the layers of the outfit will stay together.

**3.** Paint your outfit with one or more colors, being careful not to get paint on the hanger. Decorate your designer original with doilies, sequins, lace, ribbon, feathers, stickers, buttons, or fabric scraps.

Hang your creation up for all to admire.

# Puzzle Pieces Easter Wreath

Wreaths aren't just for Christmas anymore!

## Here is what you need:

4 cups of old jigsaw-puzzle pieces

white glue

green food coloring

pretty artificial flowers

yellow yarn

9-inch (23-centimeter) paper plate

large mixing bowl

measuring cup

spoon

plastic wrap

hole punch

scissors

## Here is what you do:

**1.** Mix four drops of green food coloring with a cup of white glue. Mix the green glue with all the puzzle pieces in a large bowl. If the mixture seems too drippy, add more puzzle pieces. Stir until the pieces are evenly coated with glue.

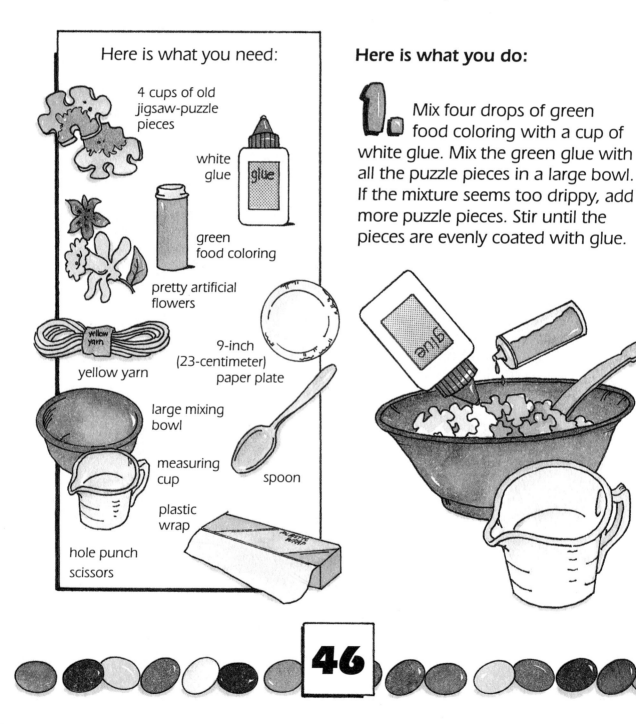

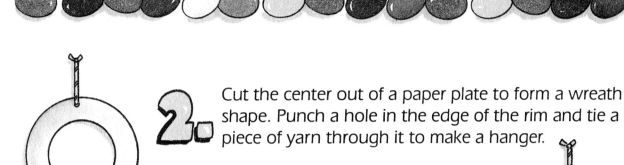

**2.** Cut the center out of a paper plate to form a wreath shape. Punch a hole in the edge of the rim and tie a piece of yarn through it to make a hanger.

**3.** Set the rim on a piece of plastic wrap on a flat surface where the wreath will be able to dry for several days without being moved. Pile spoonfuls of the puzzle-piece mixture around the rim to form a three-dimensional wreath. You may not need to use all of the mixture. Add or subtract pieces until the wreath looks right to you.

**4.** When the wreath has dried completely, you can decorate it by gluing on some artificial flowers.

What an unusual wreath!

# About the author and illustrator

Twenty years as a teacher and director of nursery school programs have given Kathy Ross extensive experience in guiding young children through craft projects. Her craft projects have appeared in *Highlights* magazine, and she has also written numerous songs for young children. She lives in Oneida, New York.

Sharon Lane Holm won awards for her work in advertising design before shifting her concentration to children's books. Her illustrations have since added zest to books for both the trade and educational markets. She lives in New Fairfield, Connecticut.